(Intermediate)

Cool Classics
Level Four

For Piano Solo
Compiled and Arranged by Wesley Schaum

Forword

This book offers a unique approach to classics for the piano student. Familiar themes by classic composers are presented in two, and sometimes three sections forming a medley. In the first section, the theme is arranged in traditional style. The second and third sections are written in contrasting and embellished versions. Many of the embellishments are lighthearted caricatures with syncopations in a jazzy style. Others are enhanced with contemporary harmonies, imaginative bass lines and counter melodies.

Students will enjoy the stylistic changes and subtle humor that makes these pieces fun to play and terrific for recitals. This series consists of three books, Level 2, Level 3 and Level 4.

Index

Title	Composer	Page
Finlandia (Op. 26)	Sibelius	13
March in D Major	Bach	8
Marche Militaire (Op. 51, No. 1)	Schubert	21
Minuet in G	Beethoven	16
Pomp and Circumstance March (Op. 39, No. 1)	Elgar	2
Romeo and Juliet, Love Theme (from the ballet)	Tchaikowsky	5
Sonata in C Major (K545)	Mozart	10
Tales from the Vienna Woods (Op. 325)	Strauss	18

Schaum Publications, Inc. • 10235 N. Port Washington Rd. • Mequon, WI 53092
www.schaumpiano.net

© Copyright 2010 by Schaum Publications, Inc., Mequon, Wisconsin
International Copyright Secured • All Rights Reserved • Printed in U.S.A.
ISBN-13: 978-1-936098-24-8

Warning: The reproduction of any part of this publication without prior written consent of Schaum Publications, Inc. is prohibited by U.S. Copyright Law and subject to penalty. This prohibition includes all forms of printed media (including any method of photocopy), all forms of electronic media (including computer images), all forms of film media (including filmstrips, transparencies, slides and movies), all forms of sound recordings (including cassette tapes and compact disks), and all forms of video media (including video tapes and DVD).

Pomp and Circumstance March
(Op.39, No.1)

Edward Elgar (1857-1934)

Romeo and Juliet, Love Theme
(from the ballet)

March in D Major

Allegro ♩= 126-132

Johann Sebastian Bach (1685-1750)

Sonata in C Major

(K545)

Wolfgang Amadeus Mozart (1756-1791)

Finlandia

(Op.26)

Andantino ♩ = 96-104

Jean Sibelius (1865-1957)

Minuet in G

Ludwig van Beethoven (1770-1827)

Tales from the Vienna Woods
(Op.325)

Johann Strauss, Jr. (1825-1899)

Marche Militaire
(Op.51, No.1)

Franz Schubert (1797-1828)